VEGAS GOLDEN KNIGHTS

BY HAROLD P. CAIN

Copyright © 2023 by Press Room Editions. All rights reserved. No part of this book may be used or reproduced in any manner whatsoever, including internet usage, without written permission from the copyright owner, except in the case of brief quotations embodied in critical articles and reviews.

Book design by Maggie Villaume
Cover design by Maggie Villaume

Photographs ©: Karl B. DeBlaker/AP Images, cover; Scott D. Stivason/Cal Sport Media/AP Images, 4–5, 7; John Locher/AP Images, 8, 10–11, 16–17, 18, 29; Erik Kabik Photography/MediaPunch/IPX/AP Images, 13; Marcio Jose Sanchez/AP Images, 14–15; Ross D. Franklin/AP Images, 20–21; David Becker/AP Images, 22–23; Jack Dempsey/AP Images, 24; Stacy Bengs/AP Images, 26

Press Box Books, an imprint of Press Room Editions.

ISBN
978-1-63494-499-1 (library bound)
978-1-63494-525-7 (paperback)
978-1-63494-576-9 (epub)
978-1-63494-551-6 (hosted ebook)

Library of Congress Control Number: 2022902465

Distributed by North Star Editions, Inc.
2297 Waters Drive
Mendota Heights, MN 55120
www.northstareditions.com

Printed in the United States of America
042024

ABOUT THE AUTHOR
Harold P. Cain is a retired English teacher and lifelong sports fan originally from Rockford, Illinois. He and his wife now live in Cathedral City, California, where they enjoy hiking, golf, and spending time with their daughter and three grandchildren in Los Angeles.

TABLE OF CONTENTS

CHAPTER 1
THE NEW KIDS
5

CHAPTER 2
DESERT HOCKEY
11

CHAPTER 3
A MIRACLE RUN
17

SUPERSTAR PROFILE
MARK STONE
22

CHAPTER 4
STAYING GOLDEN
25

QUICK STATS 30
GLOSSARY 31
TO LEARN MORE 32
INDEX 32

1

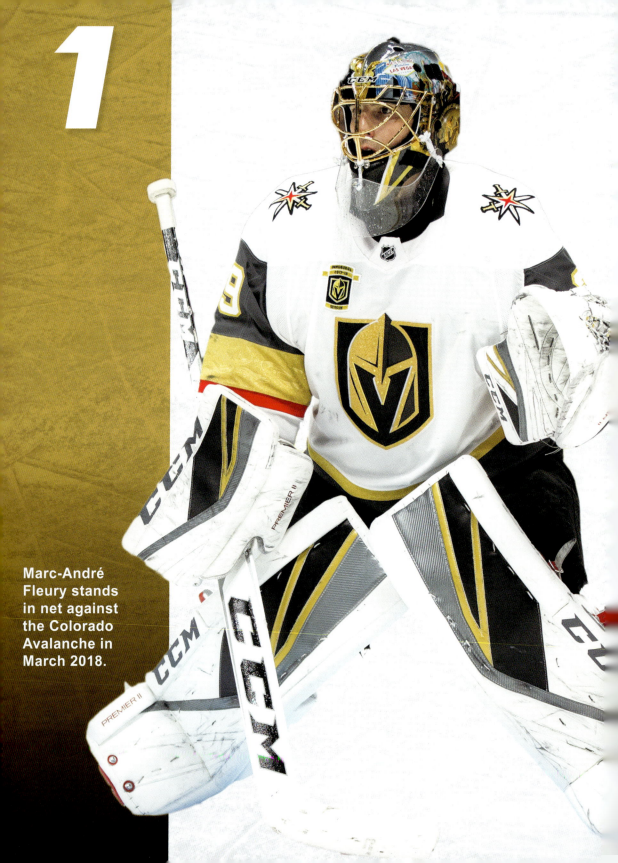

Marc-André Fleury stands in net against the Colorado Avalanche in March 2018.

THE NEW KIDS

Goalie Marc-André Fleury knew he had to stay sharp. His Vegas Golden Knights held a 1–0 lead. But the Colorado Avalanche players were buzzing around the net. The Avalanche were one of the top teams in the National Hockey League (NHL).

Colorado's Blake Comeau came in from Fleury's right. He passed the puck to Erik Johnson. Comeau bumped Fleury as he skated by. Johnson took the pass and fired the puck into the net. Vegas coaches argued that Comeau had interfered with Fleury. But the referees disagreed. The game was now tied 1–1.

The Golden Knights bounced back less than a minute later. Knights defenseman Shea Theodore passed the puck to Jonathan Marchessault in the offensive zone. Marchessault sized up the Colorado goalie. Then he ripped a wrist shot into the net. The Golden Knights had taken the lead right back.

Like Colorado, Vegas was one of the league's top teams. However, few people had expected that when the 2017–18 season began. After all, the Golden

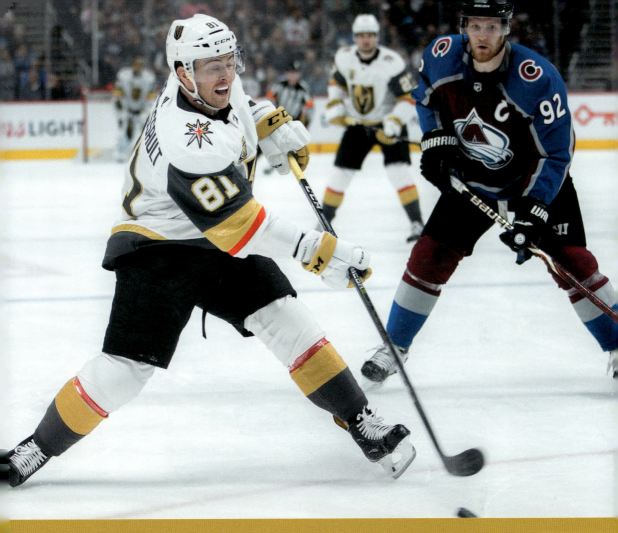

Jonathan Marchessault takes a shot against the Avalanche in March 2018.

Knights were playing their first season. Expansion teams rarely made the NHL playoffs. But Vegas had a chance to become the first to do so in nearly four

William Karlsson celebrates after an empty-net goal that clinched a playoff spot for the Golden Knights in 2018.

decades. A win in this game against Colorado would clinch a playoff spot.

In the third period, Vegas broke the game open. Theodore scored early in the period to make it 3–1. Fleury refused to allow the Avalanche to score again. As the clock ticked down toward zero, William Karlsson added an empty-net goal. It was his 40th goal of the season.

The Vegas crowd cheered as the final horn sounded. Their team was headed to the playoffs. But the Golden Knights had even bigger goals in mind.

A LEAGUE OF THEIR OWN

Expansion teams usually do very poorly in their first seasons. Between 1960 and 2018, there were 64 expansion teams in the four major North American sports leagues. Vegas was the first of those 64 teams to have a winning record in its first season.

2

Bill Foley attends the NHL Expansion Draft in 2017.

DESERT HOCKEY

Las Vegas is a hot city in the desert. Yet hockey has had a presence there for decades. In 1991, the NHL held a preseason game in Las Vegas. And starting in 1997, the Los Angeles Kings held a preseason game there every year. By 2014, businessman Bill Foley believed Las Vegas deserved a team of its own.

Having a place to play was the easy part. Las Vegas was already building a new arena for sports, concerts, and other events. Foley started a drive to see how many people would buy season tickets. He got 13,000 people to put down money toward buying tickets. The NHL was convinced. The league awarded Las Vegas a team in 2016.

Now the team needed a name. Foley had attended the United States Military

DESERT ICE

Each year on New Year's Day, the NHL holds an outdoor hockey game called the Winter Classic. But long before this tradition began, Vegas hosted the NHL's first ever outdoor game. The Los Angeles Kings and New York Rangers played a preseason game in 1991. The temperature was 85 degrees Fahrenheit (29°C).

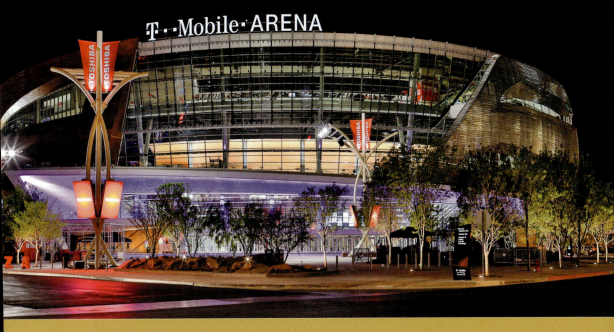

The Knights played their first game at T-Mobile Arena on October 10, 2017.

Academy, home of the Black Knights. And the state of Nevada is known for its gold mines. So, the team became known as the Golden Knights.

In June 2017, Vegas took part in an expansion draft. The 30 other NHL teams could protect a certain number of players. Then the Golden Knights could select from the players who were still available.

James Neal shields the puck in a 2018 game against the Sharks.

The Golden Knights could pick one player from each team. Typically, expansion drafts include players who are unwanted by their teams. But a few teams left star players available. Vegas grabbed veteran goalie Marc-André Fleury and high-scoring forward James Neal.

These stars made an immediate impact. The Knights won eight of their first nine games. They weren't just good for an expansion team. They were one of the best teams in the NHL.

The Golden Knights clinched a playoff spot in March 2018. Then they went on to win the Pacific Division title. And they were just getting warmed up.

3

Erik Haula celebrates a game-winning goal in the 2018 playoffs.

A MIRACLE RUN

Fans packed T-Mobile Arena on April 11, 2018. The occasion was the first playoff hockey game in Vegas history. The fans provided a level of noise that matched their excitement. And their team fed off the support. Marc-André Fleury made 30 saves and shut out the Los Angeles Kings.

Fleury allowed a goal in Game 2. But it was the only one

William Karlsson celebrates after a Golden Knights goal against the San Jose Sharks in the 2018 playoffs.

across regulation and two overtimes. Knights forward Erik Haula scored the winner in the second overtime. Vegas hit the road up two games to none. Fleury recorded another shutout in Game 4 to complete the sweep.

The Knights' next opponent was a familiar one. They had battled with the

San Jose Sharks in the division all season long. In Game 1, Vegas shocked their rivals with a 7–0 win. The Sharks battled back to tie the series at two games each. But Fleury recorded another shutout in Game 6. That clinched the series for the Golden Knights.

Vegas had to start on the road in the Western Conference Final. And this time, Vegas lost Game 1. But that was the team's only loss of the series. The Knights became just the third NHL team to make the Stanley Cup Final in their first season.

Vegas faced the Washington Capitals in the Final. And the Knights had home-ice advantage. In Game 1, Vegas scored three goals in the third period to win 6–4.

Shea Theodore gives his stick to a fan after winning Game 1 of the 2018 Stanley Cup Final.

Fans were dreaming that their team might go all the way.

Unfortunately, the team's magical run hit a wall. Washington won the next four games. Even so, Knights fans were proud of their team. They would remember this playoff run forever.

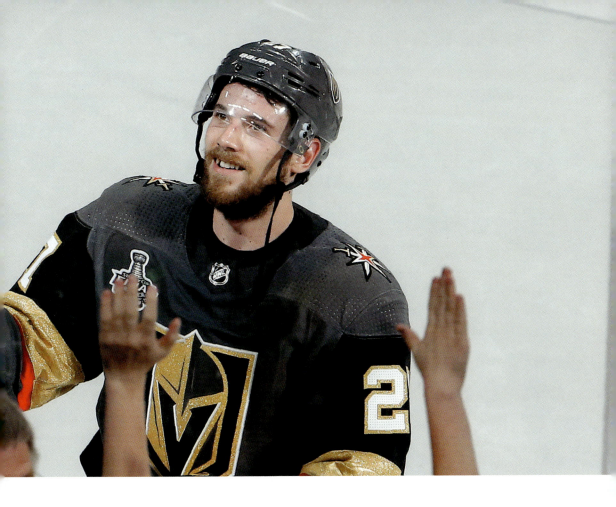

• TOUGHER ROAD

Before the Knights, two other NHL teams had made the Final in their first season. But they had an easier road than the Knights. The 1918 Toronto Arenas had to post the best record over eight regular season games. Then they had a two-game series against the Montreal Maroons to qualify. And the 1968 St. Louis Blues played only fellow expansion teams in the playoffs to make it.

● SUPERSTAR PROFILE

MARK STONE

Mark Stone entered the NHL in 2012. For years, he was a key player for the Ottawa Senators. But Stone and Ottawa could not agree on a new long-term contract during the 2018–19 season. So, the Senators found a trade partner in the Golden Knights.

Ottawa's loss was Vegas's gain. Over the rest of 2019, Stone recorded 11 points in 18 regular season games. He then scored 12 points in seven playoff games. That included the team's first playoff hat trick in a 6–3 win over the Sharks.

Stone continued to score at the same pace he had with Ottawa. At 6-foot-4 (193 cm), Stone could also play tough defense. In the 2021–22 season, he made his first All-Star Game

Mark Stone takes a slap shot in a 2022 game against the Penguins.

4

Max Pacioretty takes a shot against the Colorado Avalanche in the 2021 playoffs.

STAYING GOLDEN

Vegas hoped to finish its Stanley Cup mission. The Golden Knights brought back most of the same team in 2018–19. One exception was James Neal. He signed with the Calgary Flames. But Vegas brought in veterans Paul Stastny and Max Pacioretty. The Golden Knights also boosted their offense with a midseason trade for Mark Stone.

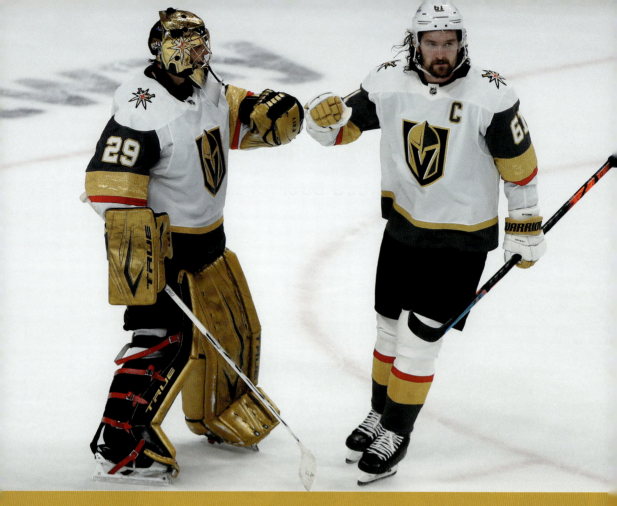

Mark Stone (right) and Marc-André Fleury celebrate after a 2021 playoff win.

However, Vegas couldn't match the magic of the previous season. The Golden Knights entered the playoffs as a third seed. In the first round, they led the San Jose Sharks three games to one.

Unfortunately for Vegas fans, the team lost three in a row to end its season.

Vegas bounced back in 2019–20. That season, the Knights won their division for the second time. But it wasn't easy. In January, the team fired head coach Gerard Gallant. And Fleury was not his usual self. Vegas traded for goalie Robin Lehner. He took over the starting job by the time the playoffs began. Vegas reached the Western Conference Final that season. However, the Dallas Stars proved to be too much.

CAPTAIN WHO?

Unlike most NHL teams, the Golden Knights opted not to name a team captain for their first season. They went without one until January 2021. Mark Stone was the first player to receive the honor.

Fleury won back the starting job the next season. He even won the Vezina Trophy as the best goalie in the NHL. The Golden Knights went on another deep playoff run. But once again, they were unable to reach the Stanley Cup Final.

In November 2021, Vegas took a risk. The team traded for Jack Eichel. The former Buffalo Sabres center was one of the best players in the NHL. However, he needed neck surgery. Some doubted if he would ever play at an elite level again.

In the 2021–22 season, Vegas missed the playoffs for the first time ever. But the next season, Eichel was fully healthy. He helped the Golden Knights return to their winning ways.

Jonathan Marchessault was named the most valuable player of the 2023 Stanley Cup Final.

In the 2023 playoffs, Vegas finally made it back to the Stanley Cup Final. The Knights faced the Florida Panthers. Eichel tallied eight assists in the series. Mark Stone scored five goals, and Jonathan Marchessault recorded four. Their play helped Vegas win its first Stanley Cup!

• VEGAS GOLDEN KNIGHTS
QUICK STATS

FOUNDED: 2017

STANLEY CUP CHAMPIONSHIPS: 1

KEY COACHES:

- Gerard Gallant (2017–20): 118 wins, 75 losses, 20 overtime losses

- Peter DeBoer (2020–22): 98 wins, 50 losses, 12 overtime losses

- Bruce Cassidy (2023–): 96 wins, 51 losses, 17 overtime losses

HOME ARENA: T-Mobile Arena (Las Vegas, NV)

MOST CAREER POINTS: Jonathan Marchessault (417)

MOST CAREER GOALS: Jonathan Marchessault (192)

MOST CAREER ASSISTS: Jonathan Marchessault (225)

MOST CAREER SHUTOUTS: Marc-André Fleury (23)

Stats are accurate through the 2023–24 season.

GLOSSARY

CAPTAIN
A team's leader.

DRAFT
An event that allows teams to choose new players coming into the league.

EXPANSION TEAM
A new team in a league, usually from a city that has not had a team in that league before.

HAT TRICK
A game in which a player scores three or more goals.

OVERTIME
An additional period of play to decide a game's winner.

PLAYOFFS
A set of games to decide a league's champion.

RIVAL
An opposing player or team that brings out the greatest emotion from fans and players.

ZONE
One of three areas on a hockey rink that are separated by blue lines.

•TO LEARN
MORE

BOOKS

Bullaro, Angie. *Breaking the Ice: The True Story of the First Woman to Play in the National Hockey League.* New York: Simon & Schuster, 2020.

Graves, Will. *Pro Hockey Upsets.* Minneapolis: Lerner Publications, 2020.

Herman, Gail. *What Is the Stanley Cup?* New York: Penguin Random House, 2019.

MORE INFORMATION

To learn more about the Las Vegas Golden Knights, go to **pressboxbooks.com/AllAccess**.

These links are routinely monitored and updated to provide the most current information available.

INDEX

Comeau, Blake, 5–6

Eichel, Jack, 28–29

Fleury, Marc-André, 5–6, 9, 15, 17–19, 27–28

Foley, Bill, 11–12

Gallant, Gerard, 27

Haula, Erik, 18

Johnson, Erik, 5–6

Karlsson, William, 9

Lehner, Robin, 27

Marchessault, Jonathan, 6, 29

Neal, James, 15, 25

Pacioretty, Max, 25

Stastny, Paul, 25

Stone, Mark, 22, 25, 27, 29

Theodore, Shea, 6